Flowers Names Book

Arum Lily

Aster

Buttercup

Daffodil

Canna

Daisy

Dahlia

Hibiscus

Gladiolus

Jasmine

Lavender

Lilac

Lotus

Orchids

Periwinkle

Poppy

Petunia

Purple Mallow

Rose

Sunflower

Tiger Lily

Tulip

Ahlan Emirate
P.O Box 5232, Fujairah Freezone,
Fujairah. United Arab Emirates